LIBBA

The Magnificent Musical Life of Elizabeth Cotten

BY Laura Veirs

ILLUSTRATED BY Tatyana Fazlalizadeh

chronicle books·san francisco

Libba Cotten heard music everywhere.

She heard it in the river when she brought in water
for her mother. She heard it in the ax when she chopped
wood for kindling. She heard it in the freight trains
moving down the tracks near her home.

She even heard it when she wasn't allowed to.
When her brother Claude was at work, Libba
snuck into his room and borrowed his guitar.

"Dang!" she whispered. Claude was right-handed.
Libba was not.

She turned the guitar upside down and played it backwards.
It was kind of like brushing your teeth with your foot.
Or tying a shoe with one hand. Nobody else played that way,
but it was the way that felt right to Libba.

Like a train plays rhythms on the tracks,

Libba made the notes go up and down.

Like water bubbles in a brook,

Libba sang a little song.

Like a girl doing what she was born to do,

Libba played the guitar, upside down

and backwards.

One time she broke a string. Another time she scratched
the wood. Each time she put the guitar back.

"DANG!" Claude said. "She's done it again."

But then Libba played him a song upside down and backwards.
She played a funny way, but she sure was good!

Soon Claude moved out to get a job, taking his guitar with him.

But Libba never stopped in her tracks.
She kept rolling.

"Now, what can a little
girl like you do?"

"I can sweep the floors. I can pick
the vegetables. I can set the table."

She earned 75 cents a month. Pretty soon she had saved up $3.75, just enough for a Stella guitar.

All day and night she played that guitar!
Long after everyone had gone to sleep, her mother
would shout, "Babe, I gotta go to work in the morning!
How about a lullaby?" So Libba put her mother to sleep,
playing upside down and backwards.

Libba played and played. And before you could say "DANG," she'd written her first song.

She wasn't even thirteen yet!

"Freight train, freight train run so fast

Freight train, freight train run so fast

Please don't tell what train I'm on

They won't know what route I've gone."

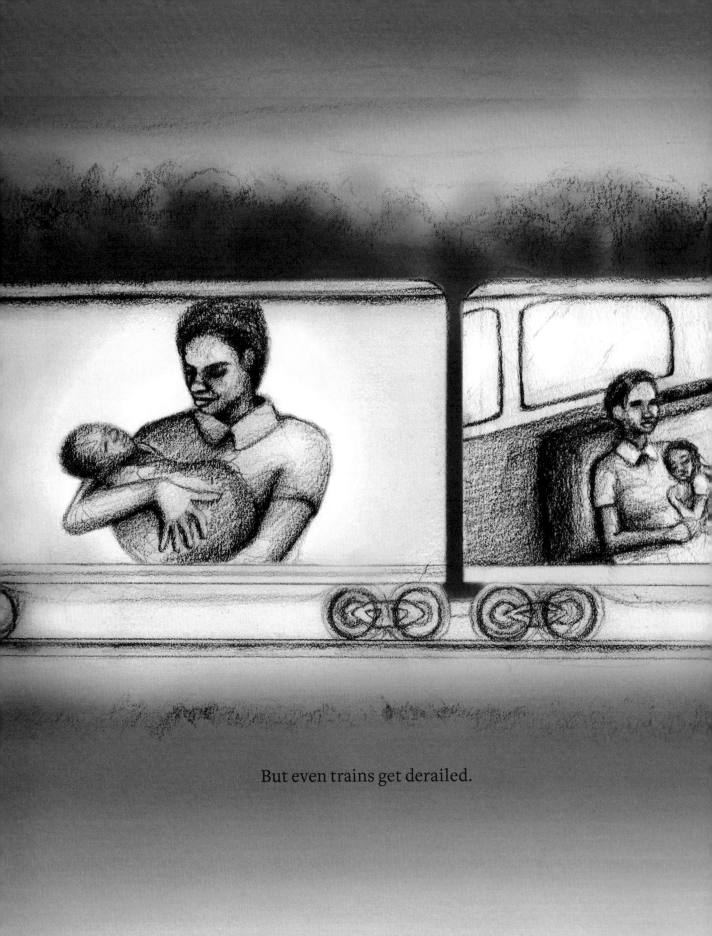

But even trains get derailed.

Time swept Libba up, and she stopped playing guitar.

Now she was a tall and stately grandmother
working in a department store. One day she
found a little girl lost in the store. She returned
the girl to her mother, Ruth Crawford Seeger,
a composer in a famous musical family.
Ruth could tell that Libba was kind and gentle.
And Libba felt the same way about Ruth.

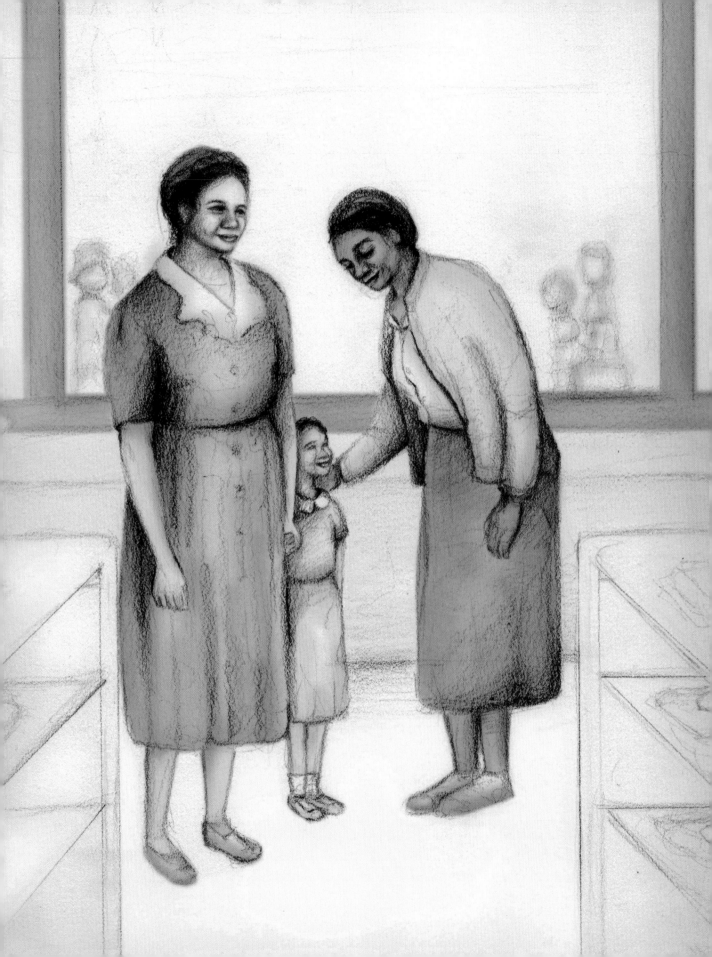

As the Seegers' new housekeeper, Libba moved like a galleon, taking care of the family. She made eight-inch chocolate cakes with six layers each. She loved the spirited children. But most of all she loved how the home was filled with music.

You could hear banjos in the bedrooms, pianos in the parlor, and bass drums in the basement. The children awoke in the morning to bluesmen and drifters sleeping by a smoldering fire. The musicians had funny names like "Lead Belly," "Woody Guthrie," and "Muddy Waters."

As Libba worked, she LISTENED.

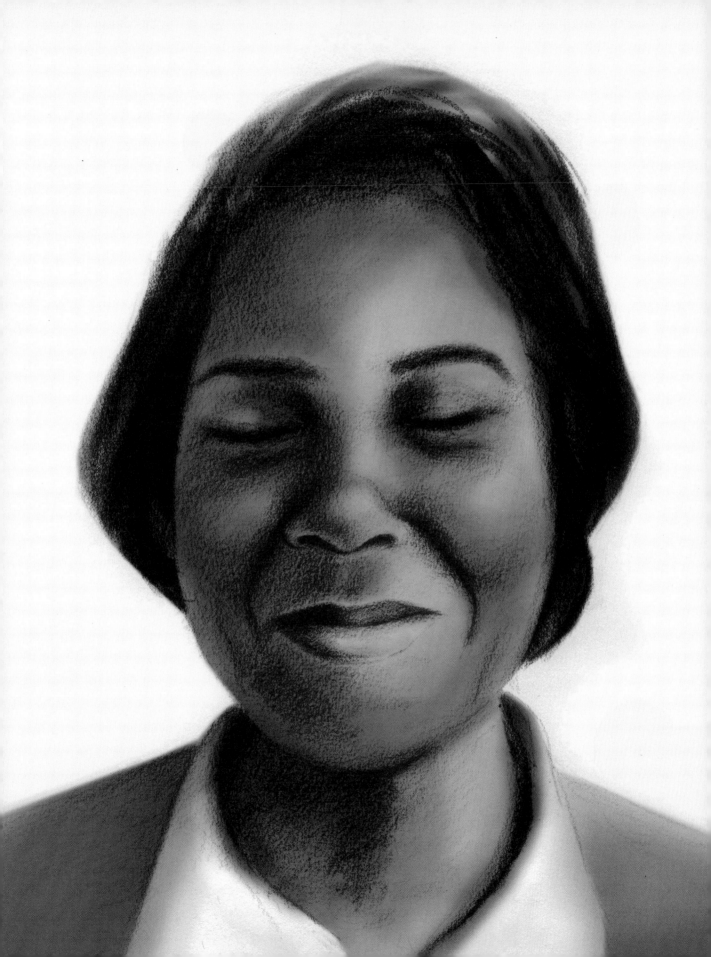

One day the kids on the porch
and the bluesmen in the living room
and the drummers down below
            heard a sound.
It was like a thousand songbirds singing.
Or a gentle spring rain.
Or a train rambling down the tracks.

It was Libba, singing and picking that guitar like she'd never set it down.

"DANG!" cried the kids.

"SHE CAN PLAY!" cried the bluesmen.

Soon the whole house was turned
upside down and backwards.
The children were clearing the dishes
and washing up.
The bluesmen were singing Libba's songs.
Ruth was playing along.
Everyone wanted to hear Libba's music.

"Sing 'FREIGHT TRAIN' again!"
they shouted.

The Seegers believed in Libba and helped spread the word about her music. But it was Libba's perseverance, her love of music, and her belief in herself that gave the world her voice.

Libba played grand cathedrals in London and velvet theaters in Rome. Thousands of people sang along when she played "Freight Train." And now, millions of people know her music.

Libba turned her guitar upside down and backwards so she could play it her own way. She turned the music world upside down and backwards, too.

Libba Cotten never stopped in her tracks.

She kept rolling.

"Freight train, freight train run so fast

Freight train, freight train run so fast

Please don't tell what train I'm on

They won't know what route I've gone."

AUTHOR'S NOTE

Elizabeth "Libba" Cotten (née Nevills) was born near Chapel Hill, North Carolina, on January 5, most likely in 1893. (It was common for poor people living in rural communities at this time to not know their exact date of birth.) She was the youngest child in a musical family. Her mother worked as a midwife and her father as a dynamite setter, among other jobs. Her grandparents were freed slaves.

Music was in the North Carolina air: People sang in cotton fields when they worked and in churches where they worshiped. Libba made up songs with her older brother, Claude, as they played by the railroad tracks near their home. When Claude was at work, Libba learned to play his banjo first, and then his guitar. Later she earned enough money to buy her own guitar.

Because she was self-taught, Libba didn't care that she was playing upside down and backwards. She learned new songs easily after hearing them only once or twice. She built up an extensive repertoire of standards, dance tunes, and rags. She became an accomplished fingerstyle player as a preteen. When she was around eleven, she wrote "Freight Train," the song that would later make her famous.

Opportunities in the early 1900s were limited for African Americans in the segregated South, especially for those like Libba who were poor and female. Libba had to work as a maid from a young age. The pastor at her church urged her to give up playing guitar, saying it was "the Devil's music." Libba married when she was only a teenager and had a baby at sixteen. (This wasn't unusual at the time.) Pressures of work and raising her daughter also prevented her from playing. As a result, it was more than forty years before she next played a guitar.

In the 1940s, Libba divorced her husband and moved in with her grown daughter in Washington, DC. Libba got a job as a doll clerk in a department store. By chance she met accomplished musician Ruth Crawford Seeger and started working as a housekeeper in the famous folk-singing Seeger home. It was here that she rediscovered her passion for music. One day the Seeger children heard beautiful music coming from the kitchen. When they went in to see who was playing, they were surprised and delighted to see it was Libba.

The Seegers helped expose Libba's music to the world. She was very close with the family, especially Mike, who she recorded and toured with for years. He recorded her first album in 1958, when she was in her early sixties, in her bedroom with her grandchildren watching quietly on. Pete Seeger featured her on his TV show. And while I took some artistic liberty in placing Libba within the velvet theaters of Rome, Peggy Seeger did take Libba's song "Freight Train" to England, where it became a hit, and where Libba later toured. Today, "Freight Train" is considered one of the most famous folk songs in the world. Libba's songs have been covered by Peter, Paul and Mary; Bob Dylan; and the Grateful Dead, among many others.

Libba recorded and toured extensively through the United States and Europe in her sixties, seventies, and eighties. She won a National Heritage Fellowship from the National Endowment for the Arts in 1984, and a Grammy the next year when she was in her early nineties. There's even a park named after her: Libba Cotten Grove, in Syracuse, New York, where she spent many of her last days, until she died in 1987.

She was also deeply dedicated to her family. She took care of four generations of children and grandchildren. When she wasn't on tour, she sang the children to sleep every night. She invited them to make up lyrics to her songs. In fact, this is how the song "Shake Sugaree" came about.

Libba was gentle, graceful, brilliant, and spiritual. Her unique style of playing coupled with her sincere love of guitar make her a beloved personality in folk music. As Mike Seeger once said about her: "White, black, man or woman, there's no one who has the tone and the rhythm and the general feeling of her songs."

∞

I first learned about Libba when I was a young child—my father used to play "Freight Train" on our family guitar. My parents both sang the song to me before bedtime. I grew to love it, and it played as a kind of soundtrack in our home.

By the time I was twenty-five, I had an album under my belt and was on my way to becoming a touring musician and professional songwriter. I began studying country-blues guitar. I was reintroduced to "Freight Train" and was surprised by the complexities of the fingerstyle technique behind this seemingly simple folk song of my youth. I was blown away when I learned that Libba Cotten was self-taught and played upside down *and* backwards. This means that she turned the guitar upside down and played it left-handed—the bass strings for her were at the bottom, towards the floor, which is technically "backwards." It was especially inspiring to watch her play in videos: As a guitar player, it was hard to imagine how anyone could play the way she did. Though it was difficult at first, I learned her song note for note. With time it became easy, and I still love to play "Freight Train" and many of her other songs.

When I had my first child, I recorded my first album of songs for children. While researching songs for the album, I discovered an amazing album by beloved folk musician Peggy Seeger called *American Folk Songs for Children*. I learned that Peggy's mother, Ruth Crawford Seeger, was a prominent folk-song collector, composer, and piano teacher in the 1950s. Her life intrigued me, and in researching Ruth Seeger, I learned that through a chance encounter in a department store, Libba Cotten became her housekeeper. This accidental meeting of two musical geniuses was a wonderful discovery—and a story worth telling.

Through my interviews with Libba's friends and family, I got to know more about what she was like. I learned about what she wore (a long dark dress and an apron at work, and later, shawls and long gathered skirts on stage) and what she liked to cook (cakes and chicken and dumplings). Everyone spoke about her kind smile, wry sense of humor, and feisty energy. It made sense to me that she toured into her nineties.

Libba believed that people could accomplish anything at any age. Her story appeals to me as a musician, as a woman, and as a fan of folk history. Libba accomplished so much despite growing up poor in the segregated South where very few opportunities were available to her. I hope readers will explore the life and music of Libba Cotten, a beautiful tributary of the great river that is American folk music.

WORKS CITED

WEBSITES:

"Elizabeth Cotten." Encyclopedia of World Biography. 2004.
Encyclopedia.com. www.encyclopedia.com/people/literature-and-arts/
music-popular-and-jazz-biographies/elizabeth-cotten

"Elizabeth Cotten: Master of American folk music."
Artist Spotlight, Smithsonian Folkways. www.folkways.si.edu/
elizabeth-cotten-master-american-folk/music/article/smithsonian

Kirst, Sean. "Pete Seeger on Libba Cotten, musical genius cast in bronze
in Syracuse." Syracuse.com. September 18, 2012. www.syracuse.com/kirst/
index.ssf/2012/09/post_324.html

"NEA National Heritage Fellowships: Elizabeth Cotten." National Endowment
for the Arts. www.arts.gov/honors/heritage/fellows/elizabeth-cotten

Pareles, Jon, "Elizabeth Cotten at 90, Bigger than the Tradition,"
The New York Times, January 7, 1983. www.nytimes.com/1983/01/07/arts/
elizabeth-cotten-at-90-bigger-than-the-tradition.html

VIDEOS:

Many videos of Elizabeth Cotten can be found on YouTube.

Elizabeth Cotten playing "Freight Train":
www.youtube.com/watch?v=dgQEOkuCRZo

Elizabeth Cotten playing "Washington Blues":
www.youtube.com/watch?v=voPJENW6i4c

Elizabeth Cotten playing "Spanish Flangdang" and "Guitar, Guitar":
www.youtube.com/watch?v=N5MTbScgKVE

Elizabeth Cotten playing "Vestapol":
www.youtube.com/watch?v=7b6sdUIG3dc

Elizabeth Cotten interviewed by Aly Bain:
www.youtube.com/watch?v=Tm5-WdB_aVE

Elizabeth Cotten interviewed on *Rainbow Quest*, Pete Seeger's TV show:
https://www.youtube.com/watch?v=HByPKQDN1AM

INTERVIEWS:

Peggy Seeger, folk musician and friend of Elizabeth Cotten, in discussion with the author, February 11, 2014.

Alice Gerrard, bluegrass singer and friend of Elizabeth Cotten, in discussion with the author, March 3, 2014.

Dana Klipp, musician and accompanist to Elizabeth Cotten, in discussion with the author, March 5, 2014.

Brenda Evans, great-granddaughter of Elizabeth Cotten and singer on "Shake Sugaree," in discussion with the author, April 5 & 6, 2017.

RECORDINGS:

Elizabeth Cotten. *Freight Train and Other North Carolina Folk Songs and Tunes*. Smithsonian Folkways. Recorded 1958. (a.k.a. *Folksongs and Instrumentals with Guitar*)

Elizabeth Cotten. *Shake Sugaree*. Smithsonian Folkways. Released 1967.

Elizabeth Cotten. *Live!* Arhoolie Records. Released 1983.

LINER NOTES:

Seeger, Mike. Liner notes accompanying *Freight Train and Other North Carolina Folk Songs and Tunes*, by Elizabeth Cotten. Washington, DC : Smithsonian Folkways, 1989 reissue of the 1958 album *Folksongs and Instrumentals with Guitar*.

To my family. —L.V.

To my mom. —T. F.

Thank you: Carson Ellis, Tucker Martine, Taylor Norman, Steven Malk, Mac Barnett, Peggy Seeger, Kim Seeger, Alice Gerrard, Dana Klipp, Becca Clarren, Johanna Wright, Susan Nevin, Brenda Evans, Alexia Smith, and Judith Tick. Many thanks to the Museum of the African Diaspora for their early support of the book.—L. V.

Library of Congress Cataloging-in-Publication Data:

Names: Veirs, Laura, author. | Fazlalizadeh, Tatyana, illustrator.

Title: Libba : the magnificent musical life of Elizabeth Cotten / by Laura Veirs ; illustrated by Tatyana Fazlalizadeh.

Description: San Francisco, California : Chronicle Books, [2018]

Identifiers: LCCN 2016049429 | ISBN 9781452148571 (alk. paper)

Subjects: LCSH: Cotten, Elizabeth—Juvenile literature. | African American women singers—Biography—Juvenile literature. | Singers—United States—Biography—Juvenile literature.

Classification: LCC ML3930.C67 V45 2018 | DDC 782.42162/130092 [B] —dc23 LC record available at https://lccn.loc.gov/2016049429

Manufactured in China.

Design by Jennifer Tolo Pierce.

Typeset in Freight Text and Freight Display Pro.

The illustrations in this book were rendered in graphite and digital color.

10 9 8 7 6 5 4 3 2 1

Chronicle Books LLC

680 Second Street

San Francisco, California 94107

Chronicle Books—we see things differently. Become part of our community at www.chroniclekids.com.

From the Mike Seeger Collection (#20009), Southern Folklife Collection, University of North Carolina at Chapel Hill. Permission courtesy of David Gahr Estate/Getty Images.

Elizabeth Cotten at home with her great-grandchildren John Evans, Brenda Evans, Linda Colbert, and Wendy Colbert (clockwise from the top).